THE THOUGHTS

OF

A

GROWING POET

BY FROST DEATH

IF THIS BOOK SHOULD EVER ROAM

PLEASE DON'T READ, SEND IT HOME

IF MY NAME YOU DO NOT KNOW

ON THE NEXT PAGE IT SHALL SHOW

THIS BOOK OFFICIALLY BELONGS TO:

NAME: _____

EXTENDING GRATITUDE TO: CHELS, GILLS & ALEX WHO HELPED TO MAKE THIS BOOK POSSIBLE. AND MY PUBLISHER WHO HAD THE MOST PATIENCE.

TABLE OF CONTENTS

HEAVEN

WHAT IS IT LIKE UP THERE?

WILL THERE BE SORROW OR PAIN

CAN HEARTS STILL BE BROKEN

OR WITH BLOOD SOMEONE STAINED

SHALL THERE BE SILVER AND GOLD
MANSIONS

WILL TAXES STILL HAVE TO BE PAID

ARE HOMES GOING TO BE FREE FOR
EVERYONE?

SO THAT NO ONE SHALL BE ON THE
STREETS

CAN WE FIND TRUE HAPPINESS THERE?

FOR BOTH THE YOUNG AND OLD

WOULD WE ACTUALLY SEE HIS FACE?

IN THAT WONDERFUL CITY OF GOLD

FORGIVENESS

A WONDER IT IS TO BE FORGIVEN

TO GET FINALLY A SECOND CHANCE

ALL TO FIX THE MISTAKES YOU'VE DONE

THEN PUT IT ALL IN THE PAST

TO SAY YOU'RE VERY, VERY SORRY

AND YOUR MISTAKE SHALL NOT HAPPEN
AGAIN

WHILE WATCHING THE PERSON'S FACE

HOPING TO HEAR YOU'VE BEEN
FORGIVEN

SO HAPPY YOU SHALL THEN FEEL

WITH TEARS RUNNING DOWN YOUR
FACE

A HUG MAYBE YOU SHALL RECEIVE

KNOWING YOUR HEARTS IN THE RIGHT
PLACE

BURNING HELL

WHAT IS IT LIKE BENEATH THERE?
UNDER THE DEPTHS OF THE EARTH
AWAY FROM THE FACE OF GOD HIMSELF
BURNING IN FIRE FOR ETERNITY

IN THAT FEARSOME PLACE OF DESPAIR
WHERE NO MAN HAS EVER ONCE
ESCAPED
AND DEMONS, MONSTERS WITH DEVILS'
DWELL
AS THEY WATCH US TURN TO CRISP

WATCH US WITH PLEASURE ON THEIR
FACES

SEEING MORTALS IN PAIN AND
SUFFERING

WATCHING THEM PLEAD FOR FREEDOM

KNOWING WELL THAT THERE IS NO
ESCAPE

TO THINK ABOUT THAT NEVER OUTING
FURNACE

THAT GETS HOTTER AND HOTTER BY
THE DAY

NEVER ENDING TORMENT, YOU'LL HAVE
TO ENDURE

AS YOUR WORST NIGHTMARES COME TO
LIFE

BUT WHAT NIGHTMARE COULD POSSIBLY
BE WORSE

WORSE THAN BEING TORMENTED EVEN
AFTER DEATH

WORSE THAN NOT BEING ABLE TO CLOSE
YOUR EYES

AND NOT BEING ABLE TO TASTE JOY

THE NIGHTMARES OF NIGHTMARES
INDEED

THAT IS WHAT IT'S MEANT TO BE

AS ALL HOPE IS LOST, PLUNGING INTO
DESPAIR

THE SECOND THAT YOU'VE ENTERED

BUT WHAT'S MORE FRIGHTENED OF
COURSE

IS THE RULER OF THAT DARK AND
DESPICABLE REALM

HIS NAME ALONE SENDS MORE THAN
FEAR

INTO THE HEARTS OF BOTH YOUNG AND
OLD

HIS APPEARANCE UNKNOWN TO THE
LIVING

YET STILL HIS FACE NONE WANTS TO SEE

FOR YOUR EYES WOULD BURN FOREVER

AND YOUR HEART FROZEN IN TIME

THAT REALM I SHALL NEVER ENTER

OR SO I HOPE IT TO BE, I GUESS

FOR THE CHOICE OF ENTRY IS NOT HIS

IN THE END THE CHOICE TO ENTER IS
YOURS

MR. NOBODY

HE STRIKES AGAIN AND AGAIN AND
AGAIN

THAT SLY AND MISCHIEVOUS DEVIL

FIRST THE DRAWINGS ON THE CURTAIN

THEN ALL THE MUD PRINTS ON THE
FLOOR

AND LIKE THE AIR, THE AIR, THE AIR

HE VANISHES SO EVER QUICKLY

AND WHAT A COINCIDENCE WE'RE HERE

SURPRISINGLY WITH MUDDY SHOES AND
PAINTED HANDS

NOT ME, NOT ME, NOT ME WAS OUR
ANSWERS IN SYNC

BUT SO GUILTY HE DID MAKE US LOOK

AND NOW LIKE A LEAKING BOAT WE
SINK

ALL BECAUSE OF THE SLY MISTER
NOBODY

NO NAME

I WAS DECIDING TO WRITE THIS POEM

AND IT WAS GONNA BE REALLY GREAT

THE WORDS CAME AND THE RHYTHM

IT'S JUST THE NAME THAT WAS LATE

I DECIDED ON TEN, MAYBE TWENTY LINES

AFTER EACH LINE, A RHYME COULD APPEAR

I HAD IT IN MY MIND YES ALL PLANNED OUT

YET FINDING A NAME WAS LIKE TRYING TO CUT THROUGH AIR.

A WALK I DID TAKE EVEN THOUGH IT
WAS DARK

WITH A CUP OF COFFEE, I MOVED ON TO
A BENCH

THUS, THERE I SAT THINKING OF A NAME
ALONE IN THE PARK

(SIGHS) YET AGAIN NOT ONE CAME TO
MIND

AS I SAT THERE IN SORROW AND VAIN

AND SO, I DID GAVE UP AND LEFT

THUS, LEAVING THIS POEM INCOMPLETE

FOR I AM SORRY IT HAS NO NAME

IN THE COUNTRY PT. 1

I WAS KEPT FROM THOSE WHO WERE
ROUGH

WHOSE WORDS LIKE A STONE UPON MY
HEAD HURTS

THEY WORE TORN CLOTHES AND THEIR
SKIN SHOWED THROUGH RAGS

THEY SPLASHED IN MUDDY PUDDLES
AND DANCED IN THE RAIN

MORE THAN LION AND TIGERS I FEARED
THEIR MUSCLES

LIKE IRON ENFORCED WITH STEEL
PLACED IN LITTLE BOYS

BUT LITTLE WASN'T THE RIGHT WORD
FOR THEM NO

AS THEY WERE WAY OLDER THAN ME A
TWELVE PLUS KID

THEY MADE MOCKERY OF ME AND OF OTHERS

COPIED OUR LIPS WALKING ON THE ROAD ALONE

LIKE DOGS WITHOUT A LEACH FIERCELY BARKING

AS WE WATCH SADLY AND PITY THEIR LIVES

CHRISTMAS IS NEAR

I THINK OF THIS DAY YOU ALREADY
KNOW

BUT I'LL STILL SAY THIS THOUGH

A VERY SPECIAL DAY IS ALMOST HERE

A DAY WHERE THERE IS A LOT OF SNOW

I'M SURE IT WOULD BE QUITE QUEER

IF YOU DIDN'T KNOW THIS DAY IS NEAR

WHEN WE HAVE FROZEN LAKES

ALL BUT ONLY ONCE A YEAR

WHEN TREES IN COLD WIND SHAKES

AND EVERYONE LOOKS OVER PAST
MISTAKES

THERE ARE NO MORE WALKWAYS TO SWEEP

SO INSTEAD, WE STAND AND WATCH SNOWFLAKES

AND WALK IN SNOW THAT'S SIX-FOOT DEEP

THE DAY WHERE MEMORIES WE SHALL KEEP

FOREVER AND EVER AS WE SLEEP

THE DAY WHERE MEMORIES WE SHALL KEEP

FOREVER AND EVER AS WE SLEEP

IN THE COUNTRY PT. 2

MY PARENTS KEPT ME FROM KIDS THAT
WERE ROUGH

WHOSE HEARTS WERE LIKE STONE AND
WORE RAGGED CLOTHES

THEIR THIGHS AND LEGS SHOWED
THROUGH THEM

AS THEY RAN WILD IN THE COUNTRY

I FEARED MORE THAN TIGERS OR LIONS

THEIR SQUEEZING HANDS ON MY BREAST

AND THEIR KNEES RUNNING UP MY
THIGHS

I FEARED THEIR VOICES THAT CALLED
OUT TO ME

EVERYWHERE IN THE COUNTRY

SMART WASN'T THE WORD NO THEY
WERE CLEVER

WAITING FOR ME BEHIND BUSHES LIKE
DOGS CRAVING FOR MY SKIN

TO EAT AND DEVOUR MY BODY THEN
SEARCH FOR MORE PREY

OUT THERE ALL ALONE IN THE COUNTRY

SUNLESS LAND

WHAT IF THE SUN SUDDENLY
DISAPPEARED AND THUS IT SHINES FOR
US NO MORE? BUT SOMETHING IS STILL
HOLDING THE PLANETS TOGETHER AND
THEY ORBIT JUST FINE, NOW
EVERYTHING IS NORMAL EXCEPT WE
HAVE NO MORE SUN, NO MORE SUN TO
WAKE UP TO EVERY MORNING, NO MORE
SUN TO BURN OUR EYES, THEN SINCE
WE'LL STILL HAVE THE MOON WILL
NIGHT BE MOVED TO MORNING SINCE
IT'LL PROBABLY BE BRIGHTER AND DAY
NOW BEING PITCH BLACK OUR NEW
NIGHT, WILL TORCHES THEN BE OUR
NEW MOON. WILL WAR CEASE AND
PEACE BE MADE, OR WILL THEY NOW GO
ON MORE VIOLENT AND THIS MISERABLE
WORLD BECOME EVEN MORE NASTY
POLLUTED AND POOR, WILL THE EAST
AND WEST BE LONELY, EVEN THE MOON
AS THEY HAVE LOST THEIR FRIEND. I
MEAN THIS WOULD NEVER HAPPEN "BUT
WHAT IF"

MARSHMALLOW CLOUDS

FLOATING CALMLY THERE
LIKE MARSHMALLOWS IN THE SKY
ARE CUTE FLUFFY CLOUDS

THE GRASS, A BLADE AND MY PINKIE

THE GRASS WAS HIGH OUTSIDE THE
WINDOW

ALREADY IT TOUCHED THE TOP OF THE
SILL

IT ITCHED EVERYONE'S FEET AND HANDS

MADE US SCRATCHED AND SCRATCHED
ALL UNTIL

DADDY LOST IT AND DROVE TO THE
STORE

THE ONE ABOUT THREE BLOCKS FROM
OUR HOUSE

WHERE HE BOUGHT A BLADE SO SHARP
AND THIN

THAT IT MADE MOM SHIVER LIKE A
MOUSE

WITHIN AN HOUR ALL THE GRASS WAS
GONE

THE PLACE WAS NOW CLEAN AND AHH
SO GRAND

WAS THE FEELING OF NOT HAVING TO
ITCH

NOT HAVING TO SCRATCH YOUR FEET
OR HAND

THERE IT WAS JUST THREE FEET AWAY

THE BLADE THAT ATE ALL THIS GRASS

AND RIGHT IN THE SHADE OF A TREE

SHE WAS THE CUTEST GIRL IN CLASS

A FOOL I WAS TO TRY TO IMPRESS

SUCH A GOOD AND FINE-LOOKING LASS

FOR YES, THE BLADE I DID PICK UP

TO TRY AND CUT WHATEVER
REMAINING GRASS

CHOP CHOP CHOP WENT THE BLADE

CUTTING THE LITTLE GRASS AS IF IT WAS
SAND

BUT OF COURSE, A HUGE STONE IT HIT

THEN BOUNCED AND TOOK HALF MY
PINKIE FROM MY HAND

I HOLLERED AS I DROPPED THE BLADE

SHE HEARD AND RAN OVER WHILE DAD
CAME

LIKE A BOTTLE OF RED WINE THAT GOT
POPPED

MY BLOOD SPRAYED LEAVING ME IN
PAIN

AND TO THE DOCTOR, I WAS TAKEN

MY FINGER WAS FIXED AS I WEPT

TO THIS DAY I'LL ALWAYS REMEMBER

WHAT A FOOL I WAS TO NOW HAVE FIVE
FINGERS ON MY RIGHT BUT ONLY FOUR
AND A HALF ON MY LEFT

WILL YOU

WILL YOU LOVE ME IF I'D DIE FOR YOU?

OR GET YOU ONE OF THOSE FANCY
SPORTS CARS

I'LL GET YOU THE COOLEST HOUSE TOO

AND THE LARGEST OF ALL THE STARS

I WILL CLIMB THE HIGHEST MOUNTAIN

SWIM THE RIVERS DEEP AND BLUE

PICK THE FRESH AND TASTY RICE GRAINS

AND BLOOD RED FLOWERS FROM THE
DUE

WILL YOU LOVE ME IF I DO ALL THESE
THINGS?

EVEN THOUGH DIFFICULT AND TOUGH
THEY BE

BUT THEN IF YOU DO UPON YOUR SOFT
HANDS A RING

SHALL BE PLACED FOR THE WHOLE
WORLD TO SEE

HAPPY BIRTHDAY

THIS DAY IS ONLY FOR YOU AND YOU
AND YOU

I HOPE YOU ENJOY IT WITH WHATEVER
YOU DO

AH YES YOU HAVE LIVED TO SEE
ANOTHER

HAVE A FUN DAY WITH FAMILY FRIENDS
AND OTHERS

AND THUS, BEFORE I FORGET HAPPY
BIRTHDAY TO YOU

MY CRUSH

SAYING SHE'S CUTE IS AN
UNDERSTATEMENT

FOR HER BEAUTY SHINES ABOVE THE
REST

AND THE LOVELY CHARMS OF MY CRUSH

HAS LEFT ME WITH A TINGLE IN MY
CHEST

MY CRUSH HEIGHT I DO NOT KNOW

NEITHER HER WEIGHT BUT LESS I CARE

FOR THOSE DON'T MATTER TO ME

COMING FROM A MAIDEN SO LOVELY
AND FAIR

HER ATTITUDE IS SO CHEERY AND FUN

AND SHE'S QUITE HONEST FOR A LADY

HER SMILE'S AS BRIGHT AS THE SUN

WHILE HER LAUGHTER ALWAYS AMAZES
ME

ONE DAY MY LOVE FOR HER I SHALL
CONFESS

WITH HOPES OF NOT BEING TURNED
DOWN

AND WHEN I'M ON ONE KNEE I PRAY TO
HERE YES

AS WE BOTH HUG IN TEARS OF LOVE AND
JOY

THESE ARE THE DREAMS OF MY FOOLISH
SOUL

AND I PRAY EVERY DAY THAT THEY
COME TRUE

FOR THIS MERE MORTAL SHALL NOT DIE

WITHOUT HEARING HER SAY "I LOVE
YOU "

ANOTHER BIRTHDAY POEM

A REALLY SPECIAL DAY IS SOON TO COME

ON THIS DAY YOU'LL HAVE SO MUCH
FUN

SO WHY NOT ADD A POEM TO YOUR
DAY

TO WHICH YOU CAN BE MORE GAY

ENJOY YOUR DAY TO THE FULLEST MY
DEAR

OF COURSE, TO KEEP THAT SMILE I'LL
ALWAYS BE HERE

I REALLY DON'T CARE IF WE'RE MILES
AND MILES APART

FOR AS LONG AS WE REMAIN IN EACH
OTHER'S HEART

I'LL ALWAYS BE AROUND TO KEEP YOU GOING

AND WATCH YOUR BEAUTIFUL SMILE AS WE'RE GROWING

JUST REMEMBER THAT YOU ARE MY DEAREST BEST FRIEND

AND I'LL LOVE YOU NOW AND UNTIL THE END

WITH ALL MY HEART AND ALL MY SOUL

FOR WE'RE TWO HALVES THAT MAKES A WHOLE

SO, ENJOY YOUR DAY MY LITTLE C

HAPPY BIRTHDAY TO YOU FROM ME

VALENTINE

THE DAY OF LOVE IS UPON US AGAIN

WHERE WE EXPRESS OUR HIDDEN
FEELINGS

AND SHOWER EACH OTHER WITH KISSES

GIFTS AND SWEETS SHALL ALSO BE
SHARING

TO THE ONES WHOSE SMILES LIGHT UP
OUR HEARTS

WHOSE LAUGHTER TOUCHES OUR SOUL

AND WHEN THEY SAY THAT THEY LOVE
YOU

YOUR ONLY REPLY IS I LOVE YOU MORE

THIS DAY WE SHALL ALL ENJOY WITH
THOSE CLOSE IN OUR HEARTS

AS WE ALL FROLIC AND DANCE TILL
NOON

THEN IN A PARK ON A BENCH
SURROUNDED BY FIREFLIES

WE KISS BENEATH THE STARS AND MOON

THE SWEET YET TERRIBLE LIE

I DIDN'T DO IT I SWEAR

SHE SAID TO ME IN CROCODILE TEARS

BUT HER VOICE WAS FADING

AND HER EYES VERY MUCH DECEIVING

YET THOSE TEARS OF LIES WERE
COMFORTING

COMFORTING INDEED FOR MY BROKEN
SOUL

TO BELIEVE THE TRUTH WOULD HURT

AND MY LIFE WOULD BE SHATTERED

SO, IN THE DARKNESS OF A LIE

I HUGGED HER AS SHE CRIED

QUIETLY IN MY ARMS EMBRACING

THAT SWEET YET TERRIBLE LIE

MOVING VEHICLE

Heading to work this morning

To waste the time away

I Realized a weirD yet true thought

As my mind was floating asTray

Don't matter how hard I try

It's impossible to write

A full poem in a moving vehicle

THE BALLAD OF A WATCH

THIS IS THE BALLAD OF THE WATCH

THAT NEVER TICKED NOR TOCKED

EVEN THOUGH SO BEAUTIFUL HE WAS

THAT WORE DARK LEATHER BLACK

WITH SILVER THREADS ON THE SIDE

AND A FACE THAT GLISTEN IN THE SUN

BUT EVEN THOUGH SO BEAUTIFUL HE
WAS

HE NEVER TICKED NOR TOCKED

AND SO, THE DOC HE DID CAME

TO TELL DADDY WHAT WAS WRONG

HE OPENED UP THE LITTLE GUY

AND SEARCH HIM ALL THROUGH

THEN HE STOPPED AND LOOKED AT
DADDY

AND SPOKE WHILE DADDY LAUGHED

OF COURSE, I DID FIND OUT

WHY HE NEVER TICKED NOR TOCKED

FOR WHEN DOC OPENED UP HIS CHEST

YEA A HEART HE HAD NOT GOT

FOR WHEN DOC OPENED UP HIS CHEST

YEA A HEART HE HAD NOT GOT

AND SO, THE DOC CLEVER WAS HE

DID PLACE A HEART IN HIS CHEST

HE TWEAKED AND TINGLE FOR A WHILE

THEN SOON COVERED HIM BACK UP

WITH A LITTLE GRIN HE TURNED TO US

WHILE SLOWLY PLACING THE LITTLE GUY DOWN

A TENSION DID FILL THE ROOM WHILE

EVERYONE AWAITED A SOUND

THEN LOW AND BEHOLD THE SOUND HE DID MAKE

THAT SURPRISED AND CALMED THE WHOLE HOUSE

SO, DOC DID LEAVE FOR HIS WORK WAS DONE

WHILE WE LISTENED TO THE LITTLE GUY GO

TICK TOCK, TICK TOCK, TICK TOCK AND TICK

THE WIND

TICKLING MY EAR LOBES

FROM THE BEHIND CHEERFULLY

THE SILENT WIND BLOWS

THE THOUGHTS OF A
GROWING KING

THIS WORLD IS LIKE A VAST WASTELAND

OF WHICH I SHALL SOON NURTURE

AND PLANT MY SEEDS WHILE I'LL WAIT

WATCHING THEM BLOOM AS I SLOWLY

HARVEST EACH AND EVERY LAST ONE

DEATH

DEATH SMILES AT EVERY LIVING
CREATURE

WHY DON'T WE ALL JUST SMILE BACK

FOR ESCAPING DEATH IS IMPOSSIBLE

A MAN MAY BE ABLE TO DODGE BULLETS

DIFFUSE BOMBS AND ESCAPE TRAIN
TRACKS

BUT WHEN THE FARMER COMES TO REAP

THE SMALL SEEDS THAT NOW HAVE
FULLY GROWN

SHALL SURELY BE HARVESTED WITHOUT
BEING FORGOTTEN

AND ALL LIVING CREATURES OF THE
WORLD BE PUT TO SLEEP FOREVER

WHEN I'M GONE

WHEN 'M FINALLY DEAD AND GONE

I WONDER WHAT PEOPLE WOULD SAY

WOULD THEY SAY HE WAS HANDSOME?

HE WAS SO CHEERY AND FUN

HE SHARED HIS CHOCOLATES AND GUM

HE WASN'T TOO SMART OR TOO DUMB

OR THAT THEY WISHED I COULD'VE
STAYED

WHEN I'M FINALLY DEAD AND GONE

I WONDER WHAT PEOPLE WOULD THINK

HE WAS PRETTY DARN QUICK FOR A KID

ONE TUESDAY HE CHOKED ON A FIG

HE'S ALWAYS CALLING RANDOM DIBS

OR THAT MY FEET SHALL NO LONGER
STINK

WHEN I'M FINALLY DEAD AND GONE

I DON'T WANT NO ONE'S IMAGINATION
GOING WILD

SO, I'LL FIX ALL MY MISTAKES

NO MATTER WHAT IT TAKES

SO, OF ME EVERYONE WILL HAVE A GOOD
MEMORY

AND ABOUT MY AFTERLIFE THEY'LL NOT
WORRY

AND THEY'LL JUST SAY REST IN PEACE
MAN CHILD

MONSTERS OF THE DEEP

THERE I SAT WATCHING THE WAVES

LIKE A MINDLESS BEAST MOVING ON ITS
OWN

UP AND DOWN UP AND DOWN IN
REPETITION

AS IF STARVED IT CRAVES THE SAND

SPRINGING ON THE BEACH WHERE I WAS

AND IT MISSES NOT, YET IT COMES AGAIN
THIS TIME BIGGER

AS A NOISY DEMON WITH RIPPLING
TEETH

IT DEVOURS ALL IN ITS PATH

TAKING IT TO THE UNKNOWN
MONSTERS OF THE DEEP WITHIN ITS
BOTTOMLESS PIT

WHAT IF I DID

THIS WORLD IS NOT OF PEACE

IT'S CONSISTED OF MOSTLY WAR

FOR WAR SHALL ALWAYS BE CAUSED

BY THE SLIGHTEST MISTAKE A HUMAN

CAN, CANNOT OR WILL DO

BUT WHAT IF I DID NOTHING

WHAT IF I DID NOTHING TO CAUSE A
WAR

SHALL IT STILL HAPPEN OR SHALL THE
WORLD

BE A LITTLE BIT MORE PEACEFUL, NO

I DON'T THINK SO FOR I ALONE CAN'T

CHANGE THIS WORLD

FOR WAR, WAR IS OF HUMAN NATURE,

LOVE CAUSES WAR, SO DOES HATE

SOME MAY SAY WE ALL DISLIKE WAR

BUT THOSE SAME FEELINGS WILL BE THE
CAUSE OF WAR

SO, WHAT IF I DID NOT HAVE FEELINGS

WHAT IF I WASN'T AS A MERE SIMPLE
HUMAN, THEN SHALL I NOT BE KNOWN
AS STRANGE THEREFORE

CAUSING WAR, A WAR ON HOW TO GET
RID OF ME,

A WAR TO SEE WHO CAN GET TO DO
RESEARCH ON ME, TO RESEARCH THE
MIND OF A MAN THAT WISHES NOT FOR
WAR

SADLY, THIS WORLD IS HOPELESS FOR AS
LONG AS HUMANS LIVE

THERE SHALL BE WAR IT'S UNSTOPPABLE
FOR WE ARE ONLY HUMAN

IN THIS MISERABLE AND MESSED UP
WORLD WITH FEELINGS OF GLASS

FEELINGS THAT CRACK WITH THE
SLIGHTEST TOUCH

DON'T MATTER THE BONDS OF FAMILY,
LOVERS OR FRIENDS

ONE SHALL ALWAYS HAVE MORE HATE
IN THEIR HEART THAN THE OTHERS
THUS STARTING A WAR.

AND SO, I ASK MYSELF, WHAT IF I DID
NOT HAVE A FAMILY, LOVER OR FRIEND

SHALL I STILL BE CAUGHT UP IN THE
MEANINGLESS FIGHTS OF THIS WORLD

WHERE THE INNOCENTS' BLOOD IS
ALWAYS SHED AND THE GUILTY SPARED

YET I FIND MYSELF WITH THE
PONDERING OF A QUESTION

WHO GAVE ME THE RIGHT TO SAY WHO
WAS INNOCENT AND GUILTY?

FOR AREN'T BOTH SIDES ALWAYS GUILTY
AS THEY ARE INNOCENT WITHIN THEIR
OWN MINDS

BUT YET ONE GOES FREE AS THE OTHER
PAINFULLY DIE

WHY, OH WHY IS IT NECESSARY TO
HAVE WAR, US DAMN HUMANS

ARE JUST LIKE ANIMALS, PREDATORS
AND PREY FIGHTING TO SURVIVE

IN THIS MEANINGLESS WORLD IN WHICH
THE WEAK MUST PERISH AS THE MIGHTY
AND STRONG SURVIVES

BUT I ASK, WHAT IF I DID NOT WISH TO
BE OF THE STRONG, YET NEITHER OF THE
WEAK

BUT A BALANCE OF BOTH SHALL I STILL
HAVE TO END UP IN A MEANINGLESS
WAR WITH MY FAMILY, MY LOVER AND
MY FRIENDS

AS WELL ALSO PEOPLE OF WHICH I DO
NOT KNOW, OF WHERE THERE FROM OR
WHERE THEY BELONG

THUS, LEAVING MY LAST AND FINAL
QUESTION

WHAT IF I DID NOT WISH TO LIVE
ANYMORE

 YET NOT REGRETTING BEING BORN I
STILL THINK ABOUT DEATH

FOR DEATH IS THE ONLY WAY TO ESCAPE
THIS ACCURSED WORLD

AND TO BE FREE. FOR THE LONGER WE
LIVE THE MORE PAIN AND SUFFERING WE
SHALL SURELY ENDURE

SO, IF DEATH IS THE KEY TO FREEDOM IS
THIS WAR WHICH I DISLIKE THE DOOR.

MONSTERS OF THE DEEP PT. 2

AS SEAGULLS FLEW AROUND, I NOTICED A
SMALL CRAB IN FRONT OF ME WALKING,
TO THE EDGE F THE BEACH AS IT WAS
SNATCHED IN BY THE OCEAN. I DECIDED
TO FOLLOW SEEING IT GO DEEPER AND
DEEPER, IN THE BELLY OF THE BEAST I
STARTED TO WONDER, WHERE DOES IT
ALL END DOES IT EVEN HAVE A
DESTINATION, HEARING THE SEAGULLS
AND WAVES ABOVE ME I CLOSED MY EYES
BECOMING ONE WITH THE SOUNDS OF
THE BEAST. AS I SLOWLY OPENED MY
EYES, I NOTICED ALL THE TREASURES,
SHIPS, SKELETONS AND ANIMALS THAT
HAVE BEEN SWALLOWED BY THE BEAST.
STILL ONE WITH THE SURROUNDING
SOUNDS MY EYES CLOSED AGAIN
REALIZING I HAVE BECOME THE PREY OF
THIS BEAST AS I SLOWLY DROWNED.

VOICES IN MY HEAD

11 O CLOCK IN THE NIGHT LYING ALONE
ON MY BED

WHILE THE RAIN POURS, AND THE PLACE
DARKENS

THIS IS WHEN I'LL START TO HEAR
VOICES IN MY HEAD

RAMBLING ON AND ON ABOUT MY
MISERABLE LIFE

ABOUT DEATH AND THE PEACE, I'LL FIND

LEAVING THIS WORLD OF STRESS AND
PAIN

ARE THE THOUGHTS THAT FLOWS
THROUGH MY MIND

LAYING IN THE DARK AS THE TIME
FLOWS

THOSE VOICES HAVE NO LIMIT THAT I'VE
LEARNED

ENCHANTING ME OF FANTASIES BEYOND
THIS REALM

AND THUS, FROM MERE VOICES TO
WORDS IT TURNS

AS I SHARE THEM WITH THE WHOLE
WORLD

SOMETIMES I LISTEN TO THOSE DEADLY
VOICES

TORMENTING MY BRAIN DOWN TO MY
VERY SOUL

BUT STILL, I DON'T MAKE THOSE WRONG
CHOICES

OF SHUTTING THEM OUT FOR THEY
KNOW ME WELL

THEY GIVE ME INSPIRATION AND
DEPRESSION

BUT I'LL STICK WITH THEM TO THE END

FOR EVEN THOUGH THOSE VOICES CAN
BE DEADLY

THOSE VOICES IN MY HEAD ARE MY
CLOSET FRIENDS

THE DAY I SPOKE WITH DEATH

STANDING ON A CHAIR LOOKING AT
THE CEILING, HOLDING A ROPE ABOVE
MY HEAD. I'D GAVE UP, I'D LOST ALL
HOPE JUST ANOTHER SECOND AND I WAS
GOING TO JUMP BUT A LIGHT FLASHED
IT WAS BRIGHT AND YET SO DARK AND
SOMEWHAT GLOOMY. A CREATURE CAME
OUT IN A BLACK CLOAK AS THE ROOM
BECAME DARKER AND ALL NOISE WAS
CANCELLED, THE CLOCK TICKING ON
THE WALL WASN'T EVEN TICKING
ANYMORE AS IF TIME HAD STOPPED, AS IF
THE WORLD HAD BEEN FROZEN. YET
WITH MY HEAD STILL UNDER THE ROPE I
FIXED MY EYES ON THE PERSON IN THE
CLOAK. TRYING TO CATCH A GLIMPSE OF
THEIR FACE, I SAW A HARD OUTLINE OF
A SKULL OR SO I HOPED IT WAS FOR I
DIDN'T SEE NO EYES OR NOSE THE EARS
WAS ALSO MISSING OF COURSE BUT MOST
OF ALL THERE WAS NO SKIN. IT'S YOU
ISN'T IT I SAID, THE REAPER HIMSELF
BETTER KNOWN AS DEATH. HE GAVE A
SLIGHT CHUCKLE AND REPLIED YES, IT'S
ME NOW HURRY AND JUMP, I DON'T
HAVE TIME TO WASTE ON A MERE
MORTAL SUCH AS YOURSELF. SORRY I
SAID ABOUT TO JUMP AND GO, BUT
THEN HE RAISED HIS HEAD AND SAID

WAIT NO, NO, NO THIS IS TOO BORING, AND IT'LL TAKE TOO LONG, LET ME SHOW YOU AN EVEN BETTER AND FASTER WAYS TO DIE COME ON NOW LET'S HURRY ALONG. WITH A FLASH WE WERE ON "THE EIFEL TOWER" OUR HEADS TOUCHING THE FLUFFY CLOUDS, THE BREEZE FELT SO COLD YET BEAUTIFUL. THIS IS MORE LIKE IT HE SAID, YOU CAN JUMP FROM HERE IT'S WAY MORE FASTER THE FALL IS ABOUT 300M DOWN. A BEAUTIFUL DEATH IN FRANCE, AND THE LOVELY NOISE YOU SHALL MAKE WHEN YOU FINALLY HIT THE GROUND. THEN HE TURNED NOTICING ME SHAKING, AND MY FACE GREEN AS I WANTED TO BARF. OH, MY AFRAID OF HEIGHTS ARE WE, HE CHUCKLED WHILE GRABBING MY HAND. THEN HOW ABOUT SOMETHING A LITTLE SHORTER LIKE THE "TOWER BRIDGE OF LONDON" IT'S A LITTLE SHORTER IF I DO SAY SO MYSELF. A DROP TO IMMEDIATE DEATH, OOH JUST IMAGINE THE MARK YOU'LL MAKE HITTING THAT PAVED GROUND LIKE A 10-POUND CHOCOLATE CAKE. I LOOKED DOWN AND STUMBLED BACK TO WHICH HE NOTICED AND BEFORE I COULD SAY ANYTHING, HE GRABS MY HAND AND SAYS, STILL TOO HIGH OKAY NO PROBLEM AND WITHIN A FLASH WE WERE AROUND THE WORLD HE TOOK ME

TO SIBERIA TO DIE OF HYPOTHERMIA, I
SHIVERED TOO COLD HE SAID AND THEN
WE WERE IN FRONT OF A VOLCANO TO
WHICH MY BODY STARTED TO SWEAT,
AHH TOO HOT OKAY WHAT ABOUT THE
NIAGARA FALLS YOU'LL DROWN TO
DEATH, HMM YOU CAN SWIM I SEE
DON'T WORRY AND WITH A FLASH WE
WERE ON A RAILROAD TRACK, THE MOST
SPLENDID HE SAID THE RAILROAD SPLAT
OOH THE CRUSHING OF BONES, AND
WITH THAT BEING SAID A TRAIN CAME
SPEEDING ALMOST UPON ME. NOOOO I
SAID SCREAMING IT ALL TURN WHITE
THEN AS I OPENED MY EYES WE WERE
BACK IN MY ROOM, I LOOKED AT DEATH,
NO I SAID WITH A SMILE UPON MY FACE.
THANK YOU BUT I DON'T THINK I WANT
TO DIE YET I THINK I WANT TO SEE THE
WORLD AND LIVE A LITTLE LONGER.
OKAY HE SAID BUT WHENEVER YOU'RE
READY TO DIE I'LL BE RIGHT HERE. WITH
THAT HE VANISHED, AND I TURNED
AROUND AND LEFT MY ROOM WHILE
THINKING, DID AND ANGEL JUST CAME
TO ME IN THE FORM OF DEATH

THE THOUGHTS OF DEATH

I KILL PEOPLE EVERY DAY, OR SO I THINK.

DO I REALLY KILL THEM OR JUST
COLLECT THEIR SOULS?

EVERY SINGLE DAY MY OLD BONES
CREAK, AS I MOVE AROUND BRINGING
SOULS INTO MY REALM.

THE SUN HURTS SO A CLOAK I WEAR, FOR
THE SHADOWS ARE MORE COMFORTING.

DARKNESS IS MY ONLY PEACE, THE ONLY
PLACE I CAN BE MYSELF

TIRED I AM BUT WHO CARES, WORKING
EVERY DAY WITHOUT REST BECAUSE OF
THIS CURED IMMORTALITY

IT HURTS NOT PHYSICALLY BUT
MENTALLY, THE THOUGHTS OF NOT
BEING ABLE TO DIE.

FOR DYING IS THE ONLY WAY TO FIND
PEACE IN THE REALM OF DARKNESS AND
THIS MESSED UP WORLD BUT UNTIL

THEN, I GUESS I'LL JUST CONTINUE MY
WORK WITHOUT FURTHER COMPLAIN.

BESIDES WHOM CARES ABOUT DEATH
OTHER THAN DEATH ITSELF

RAIN

PITTER PATTER PIT

UPON THE ROOFTOPS DANCING

THE LOVELY RAIN FALLS

SUMMER SUN

ANOTHER DAY OF SUMMER

BRIGHTLY THE SUN SHINES

CASTING DOWN IT'S RAYS

DARKENING OUR DEAR SKIN

WHILE WE WAIT IN LINE FOR ICE-CREAM

TREES

THEY GROW IN DIFFERENT SIZES

SOME SHORT AND SOME TALL

THOSE THAT GIVES US BEAUTIFUL SHADE

WHILE OTHERS PLAYFULLY SWEEP THE
SKY

DANCING IN THE RAIN BLOWN BY WIND

STRONG AND WIDE THE OTHERS STAND

AS IF NO WIND COULD BUDGE THEM

HOUSES ARE BUILT FROM THEM

SO ARE FURNITURE AND BRIDGES

THEIR STRENGTH VARIES BY NATURE

YET THEIR GROWTH IS AMAZING TO SEE

FROM A LITTLE PEBBLE IN THE SOIL

TO A MIGHTY GIANT STANDING TALL

WHILE OTHERS REMAIN AS SMALL AS
DWARVES

HAPPY AND GREEN THEY ARE IN THEIR
PRIME

YET ALL GIANTS AND DWARVES MUST
ONE DAY FALL

TURNING OLD AND BROWN AS THEY
SLOWLY DIE

SOME MIGHT JUST GO TO SLEEP FOR A
SEASON

WAKING UP BACK BRIGHT AND FRESH

WHILE THE UNFORTUNATE ONES HAVE
NO RETURN

YET I STILL ADMIRE THESE BEAUTIFUL
LIVING FORCES OF NATURE

WHICH HELPS TO KEEP ME SAFE AND
ALIVE

HMM WHAT DO YOU MEAN OF COURSE
SILLY

I'M TALKING ABOUT THE TREES

MANNERS I DON'T HAVE

SOMETIMES I FORGET TO SAY THANK YOU

AND I WON'T REMEMBER TO SAY PLEASE

WHILE BEING WRONG DOESN'T MEAN I'M SORRY

I'D RATHER PUSH THAN SAY EXCUSE ME

BUT DON'T THINK THAT I HAVE NO MANNERS

YOU SEE, IT'S JUST SO DIFFICULT TO SAY AND DO

SOMETHING I'M NOT VERY COMFORTABLE WITH

WELL YES, I COULD ASK FOR FORGIVENESS

BUT I WOULDN'T EVEN BE ABLE TO SAY P

IN "PLEASE FORGIVE ME" THEREFORE I WOULDN'T

FOR I DON'T WANT TO HURT MY TUMMY

FINE YES, I'LL ADMIT I WAS WRONG

IS A SENTENCE I WOULD NEVER SAY

FOR TO PRONOUNCE EACH WORD WILL
TAKE AN HOUR LONG

SO YES, IT WOULD SURELY SEEM

AS IF MANNERS I REALLY DON'T HAVE

BUT I'M NOT BEING WICKED OR MEAN

I JUST HAVE A HARD TIME DOING THE
RIGHT THING

SO, I ASK THAT YOU TAKE THIS POEM

AS A SIMPLE FORM OF SAYING I HAVE

AND I'M SORRY FOR WHAT I'VE DONE IN
THE PAST

NOW DON'T MINE AS I FAINT

THE VIEW

HAVE YOU EVER WATCHED THE VIEW?

FROM WAY WAY WAY UP IN THE SKY

LOOKING DOWN FROM A SWEET, COOL
AIRPLANE

AT EVERT SINGLE THING YOU PASS BY

ALL THE BIG GIANT TREES LOOKING LIKE
PEBBLES

THAT WE SEE ON A DIRT ROAD, FROM
WAY UP IN THE AIR

WHILE HOUSES ARE LIKE FINE GRAINED
SAND

EACH WITH A DIFFERENT COLOR TO
OBVIOUSLY SPARE

VEHICLES ARE LIKE CRAWLING ANTS
FROM WAY UP IN THE SKY

LIKE ANTS, SCURRYING ALL OVER THE
SANDY GROUND

WHILE SEAS AND OCEANS LOOK LIKE
RUNNING STREAMS

WHEN YOU ARE UP IN THE SKY LOOKING
TWENTY FEET DOWN

TRAFFIC JAM

BEEP, BEEP, BEEP, BEEP, BEEP, BEEP

EARLY IN THE DARN MORNING

FROM JUST SIX A.M. IN MY TOWN

THIS I WAKE UP TO AS I'M YAWNING

ON AND ON IT GOES IN REPETITION

DISTURBING THE WHOLE ENTIRE TOWN

WAKING UP PARENTS, KIDS AND BABIES

LEAVING THEM ALL WITH A TERRIBLE
FROWN

IT EASES YES IN THE AFTERNOON

AROUND THREE TILL IT'S ABOUT NOON

THOSE ARE THE TIMES THAT WE'RE
HAPPY

TILL IT'S TIME TO START CHASING THE
MOON

HEADING HOME JOINING THE LINE OF
BEETLES

TRYING YOUR BEST NOT TO FALL ASLEEP

UNTIL YOU GET HOME TO BED, THEN
NEXT

DAY WAKING UP TO BEEP, BEEP, BEEP

LIFE IN THE OPEN

[YAWN] A START OF ANOTHER POEM

WRITING FROM THE HEART OF BOREDOM

I DON'T KNOW HOW FAR IT'S GOING

BUT IT SHALL BE NOTHING LIKE THE REST

FOR THIS, EVEN THOUGH COMING FROM BOREDOM

SHALL BE EXCELLENT AND PROBABLY MY BEST

VERSES IT WILL NOT HAVE AND LINES SHALL NOT BREAK

JUST A PLAIN OLD PARAGRAPH FROM MY MIND I SHALL TAKE

MEMORIES I SHALL TURN TO WORDS ON A PAGE

ABOUT MY DAYS IN THE OPEN WITH THE BOYS

WHERE WE RAN AROUND LIKE BIRDS FREED FROM A CAGE

WHILE WE DRANK AND SPOKE FOR HOURS

LIFE WAS AWESOME OUT IN THE OPEN

THE BREEZE WAS COOL THE WATER WAS FRESH

YOU COULDN'T HAVE CAUGHT US
MOPING

FOR WE ENJOYED OUT THERE IN THE
OPEN

BEES BUZZED AND THE BIRDS FLEW

WE THEN LAID RESTING IN THE SHADE OF
A TREE

WATCHING THE SKY SO PLAIN AND BLUE

AS THE CLOUDS FLOAT AND HOURS
WENT

WE LAUGHED AND CHATTED WHILE LAID
BACK

AH LIFE WAS PRETTY DARN GOOD

RIGHT THERE WE SLEPT UNTIL DAWN
CRACKED

THEN ONWARD TO OUR HOMES WE
TROTTED

LIFE WAS PEACEFUL AND FUN

YES, RIGHT OUT THERE IN THE OPEN

I WISHED THOSE DAYS HAD JUST BEGUN

SO, I COULD LIVE IT OVER ALL AGAIN

BUT ALL GOOD THINGS MUST COME TO
AN END

AND THE MEMORIES I SHALL KEEP ABOUT
THOSE DAYS IN THE OPEN

AS I NOW CLOSE OFF MY CHAPTER

GOODBYE

GOODBYE FOR I'M NOW LEAVING

AND I'M GOING DOWN TO THE SEA

WHERE THE WIND WILL BE BLOWING

AND THE WATERS PURE AS CAN BE

OH YES, I'LL BE THE CAPTAIN OF A
WONDEROUS SHIP

IT'LL BE CLEAN AS A SILVER DOLPHIN

AND SHALL HAVE MERRY FEASTS UPON
IT

MANY ADVENTURES SHALL BE AWAITING

AS WE SLAY DRAGONS AND SEA
MONSTERS

AND STRIKE FEAR IN THE HEARTS OF THE
WICKED

OF COURSE, WE'LL ENJOY SOME SMOOTH
SAILING

WE'LL HAVE TRUNKS AND TRUNKS OF
GOLD

AND OUR NAMES SHALL BE THAT OF
LEGENDS

YES, THIS WONDERFUL LIFE I SHALL LIVE
UNTIL I'M FEEBLE AND OLD

JAIL BREAK

SSSH THE GUARDS ARE ASLEEP

QUICKLY NOW, PASS ME THE SPOON

IT'S TIME TO DIG, DIG, DIG, DIG

SO THAT WE CAN LEAVE THIS CELL SOON

HMM WAIT IT'S ABOUT DAYBREAK

GIVE ME THE POSTER, COVER THE HOLE

ACT NORMAL TELL NO ONE OF OUR JAIL BREAK

AND GET BACK TO BED UNTIL IT'S TIME

GREAT IT'S LUNCH, HIDE SOME MORE SPOONS

WE NEED NEW ONE TO KEEP GOING ANYWAY

YES, BEDTIME LETS DIG, DIG, DIG SOME MORE

PHEW IT'S FINISHED, SO IN THIS CELL WE'LL NOT STAY

QUICK CRAWL, CRAWL, CRAWL FOLLOW THE MAP

DON'T MIND THE RUBBLE JUST KEEP GOING

TURN LEFT TURN RIGHT WE'RE ALMOST THERE

YES, YES, YES, A LIGHT IS SHOWING

SNIFF, SNIFF, WHAT'S THAT WEIRD SMELL

ANYWAYS FOLLOW THE LIGHT LET'S GO DOWN

WAIT WHY ARE WE FALLING NO, NO, NO

"SPLASH" I HOPE WE DON'T DROWN

"PANTS "X 2 WHERE ARE WE, EWW GROSS SEWAGE WATER

THIS WASN'T ON THE MAP ANYWAY THERE'S A LADDER

QUICK LET'S GO CLIMB, CLIMB, I HEAR THE ALARM

AND WAIT I REALLY NEED TO EASE MY BLADDER

"PSSSS" AHH THAT FELT GREAT INDEED

NOW CONTINUE CLIMBING THERE'S A MANHOLE ABOVE

BUT WAIT WHAT ARE THOSE VOICES I HEAR

ANYWAY, PAY NO ATTENTION TO THOSE AND PLEASE DON'T SHOVE

C'MON LET'S MOVE THE MANHOLE
COVER

IT'S REALLY CREAKY GUESS IT'S RUSTED

GOOD IT'S OPEN, WAIT OFFICERS WERE
HERE

"GULP" THEY'RE TURNING AROUND OH
POOPERS BUSTED

BOREDOM

SITTING THERE WITH NOTHING TO DO

NO ONE'S DOING ANYTHING NOT JUST
YOU

THE PLACE QUIET, QUIET, QUIET, AS CAN
BE

NOW YOU'LL SEE THING YOU'D NEVER
SEE

SITTING THERE WITH NOTHING TO DO

SUN

BURNING FIERCELY THERE
MILES AND MILES AWAY FROM US
THE STAR WE CALL "SUN"

CHECK OUT THE LINK TO WORK AT:
HTTPS://DEATHFROST1234.BLOGSPOT.COM/

Made in United States
Orlando, FL
27 June 2024

48363327R00046